The Entrepreneur's Social Media Playbook

Table of Contents

1. Introduction 2

2. Understanding the Social Media Landscape 3

   2.1. An Overview of Social Media 3

   2.2. Social Media Categories 3

   2.3. Demographics and Social Media 4

   2.4. Understanding Platform-Specific Dynamics 4

   2.5. Getting Started: Exploration and Experimentation 5

3. Target Audience: Identifying Your Digital Tribe 7

   3.1. Who Are They: Demographics 7

   3.2. What Are Their Interest: Psychographics 8

   3.3. Where Are They: Online Behavior 8

4. Platform Selection: Choosing Your Social Media Battlefield 10

   4.1. Understanding Platform Demographics 10

   4.2. Evaluating Your Business Goals 11

   4.3. Content Type and Format 11

   4.4. Measuring ROI 11

   4.5. Knowing When To Pivot 12

5. Content is King: Crafting Captivating Content 13

   5.1. Muse of Words: Why Content Matters 13

   5.2. The Tale of Three 'C's: Clear, Concise, and Compelling 14

   5.3. Platform-Specific Content: Shape-Shifting in the Digital

   Realm 14

   5.4. The Rainbow of Content: Text, Graphics, Videos, and more . . 15

   5.5. The Cadence of Content: Quantity, Quality, and Timing 15

   5.6. The Magic Potion: Engagement 15

6. Harnessing the Power of Visuals and Video 17

   6.1. Comprehending Visual Content's Prowess 17

   6.2. The Mechanics of Meaningful Imagery 18

6.3. Unlocking the Power of Infographics 18

6.4. Animations: The Ultimate Storytelling Tools 19

6.5. Video: A Dynamic Experience 19

6.6. Implementing Your Visual Strategy 19

7. Building Community: The Art of Engagement and Conversation . 21

7.1. Engagement: The Critical Piece of the Puzzle 21

7.2. The Art of Conversation: More Than Hitting 'Reply' 22

7.3. Building and Nurtifying Your Tribe 22

7.4. From Followers to Fans: Deepening Engagement 23

7.5. Conclusion: The Power of Social Connection 23

8. Social Media and SEO: The Invisible Thread 24

8.1. The Intersection of Social Media and SEO 24

8.2. The Role of Social Media in SEO 24

8.3. Harnessing Social Media for SEO Success 25

8.4. Social Sharing and Backlinks 25

8.5. Infrastructure for Effective Social SEO 26

8.6. Utilization of Social Media Platforms 26

9. Grow, Analyze, Repeat: Role of Analytics in Strategy 27

9.1. Understanding Social Media Analytics 27

9.2. The What and Why of Key Performance Indicators (KPIs) . . . 27

9.3. Powerful Tools for Deep-Dive Analytics 28

9.4. Insights from Analytics-Driven Growth 28

9.5. From Data to Action: The Analyze and Iterate Cycle 29

10. Crisis Management: Navigating Through Digital Storms 30

10.1. Understanding Digital Crises 30

10.2. Role of a Crisis Management Plan 30

10.3. Identifying the Crisis 31

10.4. Framing an Appropriate Response 31

10.5. Communicating the Response 31

10.6. Learning from the Crisis 31

10.7. Taking Preventive Measures 32

11. Looking Ahead: Future Trends & Your Social Media Readiness . 33

11.1. Preparing for the AI Revolution 33

11.2. Riding the Video and Visual Content Wave 34

11.3. Embracing the World of Augmented Reality, Virtual
Reality, and Mixed Reality 34

11.4. Tapping into the Power of User-Generated Content and
Influencer Collaborations 35

11.5. Leveraging Social Commerce 35

11.6. Integrating Social Listening and Analytics 35

Your culture is your brand

Chapter 1. Introduction

Navigate the social media maze with a winning strategy! Welcome to our special report – 'The Entrepreneur's Social Media Playbook'. This report is a gold mine for entrepreneurs hungry for success in the digital kingdom. Speaking your language, not tech-jargon, it paints the roadmap to earning audience trust, converting followers into customers, and amplifying your brand messaging. The world of likes, shares, and retweets doesn't have to be overwhelming or confusing anymore. So buckle up - it's time to turbocharge your business and leave competitors wondering, 'How are they doing it?' Buy this report, and let's make the world of social media your playground!

Chapter 2. Understanding the Social Media Landscape

The advent of digital age and swift shift to the internet has led to an evolution of several platforms that enable communication among like-minded people both globally and locally. These platforms, commonly known as Social Media, have become a dominant force in everyone's lives. But what is Social Media? At its core, it is a collection of internet-based platforms that promote interaction, collaboration, and content-sharing among users.

2.1. An Overview of Social Media

Born from the ashes of early chat rooms and forums, Social Media platforms have progressively become complex systems, designed with the simple goal: to connect individuals and groups instantly and effortlessly. But today, they have evolved to become a key part of our social infrastructure, shaping opinions, creating trends, and even influencing global politics.

Prominent platforms such as Facebook, Instagram, Twitter, LinkedIn, and YouTube, just to name a few, each offer unique features, audience demographics, and practices that set them apart. Distinguishing each platform's strengths and understanding how its users engage with content is an essential first step for any savvy entrepreneur looking to enter the social media arena.

2.2. Social Media Categories

Various categories exist within the wide universe of social media, each targeting a specific type of interaction or content. Here's a summary of the primary categories:

- **Social Networks**: Services like Facebook and LinkedIn where people connect with friends or business associates.

- **Media Sharing Networks**: Services like Instagram and YouTube where users upload photos or videos.

- **Discussion Networks**: Services like Reddit where people discuss a range of topics.

- **Bookmarking and Content Curation Networks**: Services like Pinterest where people find, save, and share content.

- **Consumer Review Networks**: Services like Yelp where people share their reviews about businesses.

- **Blogging and Publishing Networks**: Services like Medium where people publish their blog posts.

Understanding why and how people use these networks can help you plan more effectively to meet your audience where they are already spending their time.

2.3. Demographics and Social Media

Before diving into the specifics of each platform, it is critical to understand who is using social media. Social media usage spans across all ages, genders, income levels, and education levels, although some networks may skew towards certain demographics more than others. Data from reputable sources such as Pew Research can provide insights into how different groups use social media. To succeed, you need to develop content that is geared toward your intended audience.

2.4. Understanding Platform-Specific Dynamics

Rapid deployment of new features and frequent algorithm updates across social media channels make keeping up with social media's ever-changing landscape a full-time job. Here, we will delve into some of the biggest players in the scene, delving into their unique attributes, ideal uses, and key demographics.

- **Facebook**: The largest of all social media, Facebook boasts users of all ages. A vast bowl of diverse demographics, always bustling with activity. It offers opportunities for both organic interactions and paid advertisements.

- **Instagram**: A haven for younger generations, Instagram is image and video-centric, perfect for visually engaging content. Ease of discovery through hashtags makes it an entrepreneur's favourite.

- **Twitter**: A rapid-fire platform, Twitter thrives on timely updates and trending discussions. An ideal place for brands to showcase their wit, poke fun, or make serious political comments.

- **LinkedIn**: The ⬚go-to⬚ platform for professionals and B2B interactions. LinkedIn's user base encompasses high-income earners and college-educated individuals. Perfect for sharing industry-focused content and for networking.

- **YouTube**: As the second largest search engine, YouTube sees a broad demographic of users seeking video content. It offers brands space to create long-form content and ads that run before other videos.

2.5. Getting Started: Exploration and Experimentation

Understanding the social media landscape isn't an academic exercise, but a dynamic exploration. It would be best if you were prepared to experiment, to delve into the different platforms, try out their features, keep an eye on the latest trends, and adapt rapidly to changes. Remember, what's popular today can quickly become yesterday's news. A successful entrepreneur will not be afraid of trial and error, and he/she will be agile, ready to change course on a dime.

This chapter was meant to provide you with a general understanding of the social media landscape - the where, what, who, and how. As we dive deeper into specific aspects of social media strategy in upcoming chapters, remember that every business is unique. No one-size-fits-all strategy exists, and your success will ultimately depend on understanding your unique context within this landscape and how well you can navigate it.

With this foundation, you are now equipped to proceed further - to identify your digital tribe, to choose your battlefield, and to craft captivating content that compels and converts. The world of likes, shares, and retweets is now yours to conquer.

Chapter 3. Target Audience: Identifying Your Digital Tribe

Understanding your target audience forms the very backbone of any successful social media strategy. A digital tribe isn't something one simply stumbles upon, it is something that is meticulously constructed, polished, and subsequently engaged with. This laborious journey includes understanding your customer demographics, psychographics, behaviors, and preferences, which then sets the stage for critical decisions down the line - from platform selection to developing content types.

3.1. Who Are They: Demographics

Demographics refer to the measurable characteristics of your target audience. Think age, location, gender, income, education, and occupation. The target audience for a luxury car brand will look dramatically different from a student loan company, so understanding these differences is essential. Let's break these down:

1. Age: Generally, social media users are younger, although the users' age range can dramatically differ between platforms. Always remember to consider how your product or service falls into these age categories, and where your audience likely lies.

2. Location: Certain platforms may be more prevalent in specific areas, and platforms that might seem irrelevant in one location might be widely popular in another.

3. Gender: Understanding the gender preferences for different platforms will guide your audience targeting and content planning.

4. Income, Education, and Occupation: Higher income and education levels can suggest preferences for certain forms of

content or sophisticated messaging and vice versa.

3.2. What Are Their Interest: Psychographics

Demographics are incomplete without psychographics - the qualitative information about your audience's values, attitudes, interests, and personality traits. Psychographics help us understand why a customer behaves the way they do and offer deeper insights, enabling personalized content creation.

1. Values and Attitudes: Do your customers value sustainability? Are they more status-conscious, or do they believe in minimalism? Answers to these questions will heavily influence content production and platform selection.

2. Interests and Activities: What binds your audience together? Is it a love for vegan food, hiking, or tech gadgets?

3. Personality: Are your customers risk-takers or more conservative? High energy or more relaxed?

3.3. Where Are They: Online Behavior

Understanding online behavior is perhaps the most challenging part of audience identification. Mapping your audience's social media behaviors helps when tailoring content to match their consumption habits.

1. Preferred Platforms: Where is your audience most active online? What type of content do they typically interact with on these platforms?

2. Online Activities: What are their browsing and purchasing

habits? Do they use social media for research or purely for entertainment?

3. Timing: When are your audience members most active online? Timing your posts to correspond with these active periods can dramatically increase engagement rates.

With this detailed understanding of your audience, you create your digital tribe, carving a niche for your brand in the vast social media ocean. From platform selection to content creation, knowing your tribe is the first step towards navigating the complex social media labyrinth successfully. A target audience isn't merely a demographic or a statistic, but a living, breathing community ready to engage with your brand. Strengthen your understanding of them, and you pave the way for a stronger brand presence, captivating content, and ultimately, a successful digital campaign. Hopefully, this comprehensive walkthrough has shed some light on the power of audience targeting and its importance in your social media strategy.

Chapter 4. Platform Selection: Choosing Your Social Media Battlefield

The journey into the world of social media is akin to stepping onto a battlefield. The secret sauce to ensuring you're on the winning side is choosing the right platforms to build your presence on. The correct selection won't just influence your overall reach, but will also dictate the engagement level, type of content, and demographics of the audience you'll interact with.

4.1. Understanding Platform Demographics

Every social media platform is unique, housing a different demographic of users and varied types of content. Facebook users primarily skew towards a slightly older demographic, making it great for content that appeals to an older audience. Instagram leans towards the younger crowd, and it thrives on visual storytelling through photographs and short-form videos. Twitter, with its bite-sized content, complements businesses who wish to communicate concisely and engage in timely and topical conversations. LinkedIn caters to a professional audience who are looking to network, making it perfect for B2B enterprises. YouTube, on the other hand, hosts longer form content and fits businesses with visually rich and informative content to share. Pinterest appeals to niche interests and DIYers. Therefore, understanding who is on what platform is critical to aligning your brand with the most appropriately populated social media universe.

4.2. Evaluating Your Business Goals

Before committing to a platform, you need to introspect and map out what your long-term business goals are. Do you want to create brand awareness? Improve brand loyalty? Increase website traffic? Each platform provides something unique to offer towards these goals. For instance, Twitter's real-time content distribution can boost brand awareness, whereas Facebook's robust community features can fortify brand loyalty. Instagram, with its shoppable posts, can drive traffic to your online store, while LinkedIn's professional audience provides prime networking opportunities for B2B entities. Sitting down and understanding your goals can also help identify where your audience is likely to be and assist you in choosing an appropriate platform.

4.3. Content Type and Format

Every platform thrives on a specific type of content, be it text, image, video, or a combination. Consequently, it is essential to consider what kind of content best showcases your product or service. Instagram is built for visually appealing content and is ideal for brands that communicate well through images or videos. YouTube is a platform for longer videos that can range from tutorials to webinars or event broadcasts. Facebook and LinkedIn support all types of content, but favor informative and engaging posts. Twitter is perfect for quick, catchy statements and topical discussions. Hence, understanding what each platform emphasizes will help you tailor content that resonates with its audience.

4.4. Measuring ROI

Understanding how to measure the return on investment (ROI) from a social media platform is essential. While likes, shares, retweets, and comments are great, they do not necessarily translate to actual sales or address brand objectives. It's imperative to set up robust analytics processes to track and measure the right Key Performance Indicators (KPIs) for your chosen platform. Every platform provides its set of analytics that track different metrics. Facebook provides "Page Insights," Instagram has "Instagram Insights," and LinkedIn offers "Analytics" of varying depth. Start by understanding what KPIs matter to your business and utilize the analytics tool specific to your platform of choice.

4.5. Knowing When To Pivot

Finally, it's key to always keep a finger on the pulse of the social atmosphere, ready to pivot when required. Social media platforms evolve constantly, bringing in new demographics or losing old ones, changing algorithms and post ranking factors, and even adjusting business policies. Therefore, it's important to realize when a platform isn't delivering the results you're after. You might need to consider diversifying your presence, adjusting tactics, or even exiting a platform if it proves detrimental to your brand image. Staying flexible is considerably influential to long-term social media success.

In conclusion, choosing the right social media battlefield for your business is a combination of understanding your audience demographics, business goals, preferred content format, ability to measure ROI, and the agility to adjust as required. It might seem daunting initially, but with a robust strategy, you can conquer the digital realm one platform at a time. Remember, the platform, where your audience spends the most time and engages the most directly with your type of content, is your key to unlocking social media success.

Chapter 5. Content is King: Crafting Captivating Content

In the alluring world of social media, content truly is the majestic king who sits on the digital throne, wielding an influence as potent and vast as any kingdom. This chapter will serve as your comprehensive guide to understand, strategize, and craft compelling content that ensnares your audience's attention, drives engagement, and ultimately, promotes your brand's growth.

5.1. Muse of Words: Why Content Matters

To appreciate the kingly stature of content, let's first decipher its significance. The content you share is the essence of your brand's narrative. It communicates your brand's purpose, ethos, and offering in a language that resonates with your audience. While eye-catching visuals may initially draw wandering eyes, it is the meat of the content that sustains attention - an enamoring story, valuable information, or a captivating argument. It is this meat that the consumers digest, remember, and share, creating a ripple effect, magnifying your brand's reach and reputation.

Remember, though, that the king is only as strong as his court. In the world of content, this court is your target audience. It is their needs and desires that beget the might of your content. Therefore, your content should be a sacred chalice holding answers to their queries, solutions to their problems, and insights into their interests.

5.2. The Tale of Three 'C's: Clear, Concise, and Compelling

The intersection of these three 'C's should be your locus while creating content. Content that is clear leaves no room for confusion and firmly establishes your brand's message in the audience's minds. Conciseness is vital in the current era where consumers' attention spans are dwindling rapidly amidst a deluge of information. They crave information that is easy to consume, digest, and remember. Lastly, compelling content is that which stirs emotions, prompts thought, and compels action - be it a like, share, comment, or a purchase.

But weaving the enchanting tale of three 'C's is just the beginning. The content must adapt to the altering landscapes of different social media platforms while wooing diverse audience segments.

5.3. Platform-Specific Content: Shape-Shifting in the Digital Realm

Just as a skilled diplomat understands and respects the differing cultures of various countries, a savvy content creator must tailor the content to fit the idiosyncrasies of each platform. For instance, brevity reigns supreme on Twitter, storytelling is Instagram's muse, while LinkedIn prizes professionally oriented, industry-specific content.

Audit the platforms where your brand has a presence, learn their language, nuances, and user expectations - and craft your content, accordingly. Remember to pepper your content with hashtags on Instagram and Twitter to expand its reach, tag relevant profiles when appropriate, and use SEO-friendly keywords across platforms for searchability.

5.4. The Rainbow of Content: Text, Graphics, Videos, and more

Content isn't just limited to text - it's a vibrant array of text, graphics, videos, GIFs, memes, infographics, webinars, podcasts, and even user-generated content. Diversify your content mix to cater to different preferences and scenarios. Back up your blog posts with infographics, augment your product stories with videos, and engage audiences with quizzes or polls. Think of it as your banquet to captivate and cater to the myriad tastes of your audience while retaining the essence of your brand message.

5.5. The Cadence of Content: Quantity, Quality, and Timing

While crafting content, it is essential not just to focus on 'what' but also 'how much' and 'when.' Being consistent with the quality and frequency of your content fosters familiarity and trust, plus it provides fuel for the algorithms that push your content onto viewers' feeds. However, avoid the temptation of quantity over quality. Each piece of content should add value, not just contribute to the noise. As for timing, consider your audience's schedule and patterns. Use analytics to understand when they are most active and schedule your content timeline accordingly.

5.6. The Magic Potion: Engagement

The ultimate goal of your content isn't just visibility but active participation from your audience. Ask questions in your posts, invite opinions, respond to comments, encourage user-generated content, or hold contests. The more you interact, the more you humanize your brand, which fosters a sense of community and loyalty.

In the vast kingdom of social media, content is your ambassador and weapon. Weave it with care, wield it with skill, and win the loyalty of your subjects. Remember, every kingdom starts with a story - make yours worth telling.

Chapter 6. Harnessing the Power of Visuals and Video

Visual storytelling is an indispensable part of any successful social media strategy. Accruing substantial research, it has been discerned that visual content captivates audience attention considerably more efficiently than its text-based counterparts. Consequently, harnessing the power of visuals and video can profoundly augment the reach, impact, and efficacy of your social media presence.

6.1. Comprehending Visual Content's Prowess

Images, infographics, animations, and videos are some examples of what constitutes visual content. They all perform exceedingly well in engaging audiences. Statistics suggest posts with visuals generate 94% more total views and engagement than those without. Moreover, the human brain processes visuals 60,000 times faster than text, making it an effective tool to quickly grasp attention and convey information.

In this age of dwindling attention spans and information overload, a well-designed infographic can be a refreshing sight. Similarly, dynamic and engaging videos tend to be more immersive and interactive, keeping the audience locked in, while animations appeal to the universal human love for storytelling. In essence, understanding these details uncovers why implementing visuals is non-negotiable for a thriving online presence.

6.2. The Mechanics of Meaningful Imagery

Images play a crucial role in brand building and storytelling. They should be relevant, aesthetically pleasing, and carry the brand's tonality consistently across all platforms. They should be able to instantly trigger brand recall. For instance, using consistent filters, colors or themes can help your audience identify your brand in an instant and create a strong memory tie.

With the rise of platforms like Instagram and Pinterest, businesses have had to adapt to this visually-driven market. A well-chosen image can provoke emotion, inspire action or even educate. High-quality images reflect positively on your brand and can confidently shoulder the responsibility of conveying brand ethos and conveying pivotal messages.

6.3. Unlocking the Power of Infographics

Infographics are effective tools to simplify complex data or information and transform it into an engaging narrative. They engage viewers on multiple levels with their blend of text, images, and design. They're easily shareable across platforms and can significantly increase your reach.

Making infographics that are both informative and attractive requires an understanding of data visualization and graphic design. They should offer valuable insights while also being visually pleasing and easy to digest.

6.4. Animations: The Ultimate Storytelling Tools

Animations can be incredibly engaging tools for businesses. They can encapsulate complicated concepts in easy-to-understand, fun-to-watch videos. Do not be dissuade that animations are only for younger audiences. When employed strategically, they have proven equally effective for mature, professional crowds too.

Incorporating animated content into your social media strategies can involve a range of options. From short GIFs to detailed explainer videos, the animation genre provide immense creative freedom to narrate your brand story effectively.

6.5. Video: A Dynamic Experience

Video content is rapidly becoming the most engaging content type on social media. According to predictions, videos will account for over 82% of all internet traffic by 2022. They offer a dynamic experience, keeping the user engaged for longer periods.

Live videos, webinars, tutorials, behind-the-scenes footage, client interviews, product demonstrations-- the possibilities with video content are endless. Adding subtitles or captions to your videos will make them more accessible and user-friendly.

6.6. Implementing Your Visual Strategy

A foolproof visual content strategy should be platform-specific, as each platform favors different types of visual content. What works for Instagram might not perform well on LinkedIn, for example. Testing different types of content, analyzing the results, and refining your strategy based on the insights gained will help you tap into the potential of visual content.

Lastly, ensure each piece of your visual content aligns with your brand's tone, style, and messaging. This will not only grant your content a uniform appearance but also enhance your brand recognition and trust.

In essence, a well-executed visual strategy can cut through the digital noise, engage your audience, and measurably uplift your social media success.

Chapter 7. Building Community: The Art of Engagement and Conversation

Creating an engaging and interactive community on social media is paramount to the success of your business, and this chapter presents an in-depth approach to nurturing such a community. Social media isn't merely a platform for pushing products or services; it's a space to connect, converse, and create lasting relationships with your audience. From understanding the importance of engagement to devising conversational strategies, we delve into the artistry of community building here.

7.1. Engagement: The Critical Piece of the Puzzle

Engagement is the glue that holds your social media strategy together. It is the process through which you build a relationship with your audience, encouraging interaction and participation in your social media activities. Engagement can take many forms - liking a post, leaving a comment, sharing your content, or even sending you a direct message. Each of these interactions holds value and contributes to the sense of community around your brand.

Encouraging engagement shouldn't be an afterthought. It is crucial to weave engagement-promoting dynamics into every piece of content you produce. Ask open-ended questions to invite responses, use calls to action to encourage likes or shares, and always make a point of responding to comments and direct messages promptly. Regular interaction and conversation show that you value your audience's input and foster a sense of inclusion that is critical to community building.

7.2. The Art of Conversation: More Than Hitting 'Reply'

Fostering meaningful conversation goes beyond the basic 'reply' or 'like.' It involves empathetic listening, understanding the person behind the comment, and responding genuinely. This approach creates a stronger relationship between your brand and your audience, transforming followers into true brand advocates.

When you respond to a comment or message, try to personalize your response as much as possible. Using the person's name and referencing specifics from their comment can go a long way to building rapport. Moreover, never shy away from engaging in conversations that arise organically from your posts. These unplanned discussions can often lead to deeper connections and understanding.

7.3. Building and Nurtifying Your Tribe

Your social media followers aren't just customers or potential leads; they form your 'digital tribe'. Like any community, your tribe has shared interests, values, and goals, and as the tribe leader, it's your role to foster these commonalities. Share content that matters to your audience, build narratives around your brand that resonate with their experiences, and ensure your brand ethos aligns with the values your tribe holds dear.

An effective tribe nurturing strategy involves consistently providing value to your community. This could be in the form of educational content, exclusive deals, or even simple social interactions where you check in on your followers. Regularly showing up for your tribe positions you as a reliable, trustworthy leader, consolidating your followers into a closely-knit social media community.

7.4. From Followers to Fans: Deepening Engagement

With a digital tribe in place, the next step is deepening that engagement, turning followers into fans, and fans into brand advocates. You can achieve this by adopting advanced engagement strategies such as user-generated content campaigns, hosting live Q&A sessions, or arranging contests and giveaways. These strategies have a dual effect: increasing engagement and spreading brand awareness through shares and mentions.

Remember, building a community doesn't happen overnight. It's a long-term strategy that requires dedication, creativity, and responsiveness. Your community is a living, breathing entity - treat it with the respect and attention it deserves, and it will reward you with unwavering support, boosting your brand to unimagined heights on the social media landscape.

7.5. Conclusion: The Power of Social Connection

In this digital age, the power of social connection cannot be underplayed. A thriving social media community can act as a potent marketing resource, grow your brand's reach, and substantially boost your online credibility. Engagement and conversation are not mere tactics; they form the beating heart of any successful social media strategy. So, immerse yourself, communicate genuinely, and build a strong, engaging community around your brand. Therein lies the key to truly mastering the social media maze.

Chapter 8. Social Media and SEO: The Invisible Thread

The intertwining of social media and Search Engine Optimization (SEO) is a nuance that often goes unnoticed, yet it is a key player in digital marketing success. This relationship, often referred to as the 'invisible thread', is a potent force that entrepreneurs must understand to leverage their social media strategy efficiently. This chapter aims to provide an expansive understanding of this association and will unearth the strategies to leverage it.

8.1. The Intersection of Social Media and SEO

Though the connection between social media and SEO may seem unclear at first, it's important to recognize the influential role that social channels play in modern search engine algorithms. While social media shares and likes don't directly affect SEO rankings, the online visibility that social media provides can undoubtedly influence rankings. It fosters increased traffic, engagement, and brand recognition - factors that search engines consider when determining the relevancy and authority of a page. Google has openly stated that it considers social signals as a part of its ranking algorithm, clarifying this somewhat nebulous area.

8.2. The Role of Social Media in SEO

Social media contributes to SEO in ways more than one. It allows businesses to populate search engine results with their content, creating a stronger digital footprint. Furthermore, the amplification of your content on social media encourages more inbound link possibilities, which indirectly boost SEO. Given enough shares and likes, your content can significantly snowball in exposure, garnering more clicks and links in the process. This can, in turn, improve your SEO since the quantity and quality of inbound links to a site are strong ranking factors for search engines.

8.3. Harnessing Social Media for SEO Success

To leverage social media for SEO, you need a smart approach. First and foremost, optimize your social media profiles with your brand name and keywords relevant to your industry. Search engines index social media profiles, making them a part of search engine results. Hence, optimization ensures search visibility and adds another way for users to discover your brand, thereby increasing your brand's online footprint.

Moreover, it's important to produce shareable, quality content on social media platforms. When this content is shared, it'd reach a larger audience, thereby generating more traffic, improving your site's chances of gathering quality backlinks, and consequently enhancing your SEO.

8.4. Social Sharing and Backlinks

Social sharing can lead to increased backlinking to your website, directly impacting your SEO and search engine rankings. Backlinks or unidirectional hyperlinks are a valuable component of SEO as they indicate the credibility and authenticity of your content. The more shares your content receives, the more likely it is to be seen by content creators who could potentially link to your content from their own websites or blogs.

8.5. Infrastructure for Effective Social SEO

Another critical element of the social SEO strategy is the infrastructural aspect. By integrating social media buttons on your website, you can encourage visitors to share your content, thereby increasing its visibility and likelihood of additional backlinks. Your followers on social platforms can potentially turn into your site's promoters, especially if you are consistently providing valuable and shareable content.

8.6. Utilization of Social Media Platforms

Different social media platforms serve different purposes and audiences. Therefore, it's essential to tailor your use of platforms according to where your target audience is and what content format fits best. For instance, LinkedIn is great for B2B businesses while visually-alluring content can drive considerable SEO value on platforms like Instagram or Pinterest.

In conclusion, understanding the integration of social media and SEO provides you with a powerful tool in your arsenal. This 'invisible thread' places you in the position to generate more traffic, create a larger online footprint, and ultimately, rank higher on search engine results. The intersection of SEO and social media is far from a straight line, but once mastered, it becomes a pivotal part of your online success story.

Chapter 9. Grow, Analyze, Repeat: Role of Analytics in Strategy

As a social media marketer, it is paramount to understand that every step you take in your digital journey must have a solid rationale behind it. That's where analytics comes into play. In this chapter, we will unpack the complex and multifaceted process of social media analytics, and how it plays a critical role in shaping up your marketing blueprint and tracking its success.

9.1. Understanding Social Media Analytics

Social media analytics is not a mere number-crunching tool. Instead, it uncovers the meaningful patterns hidden behind these numbers, offering actionable insights to improve your strategy. It involves collecting and analyzing data from social networks to monitor user behavior, engagement rates, content performance, and other key performance indicators (KPIs). With a data-driven approach, you can focus on what works instead of shooting in the dark.

9.2. The What and Why of Key Performance Indicators (KPIs)

KPIs are quantifiable outcomes that help in gauging the efficacy of your social media strategy. Depending upon your business goals, KPIs could be the number of likes, shares, comments, followers, click-through rates, overall reach, impressions, website traffic, and so on. KPIs tell you where you're standing and how far you need to go to achieve your overarching objective.

To define your KPIs, follow the SMART framework: Specific, Measurable, Achievable, Relevant, and Timely. Each KPI should align with your core business objectives and help measure progress toward achieving them.

9.3. Powerful Tools for Deep-Dive Analytics

Several efficient tools promise a seamless analytics experience, from basic in-app analytics offered by social platforms to sophisticated third-party applications like Hootsuite, Sprout Social, or Buffer. They can provide granular insights into your audience demographics, engagement metrics, best-performing content, ideal posting times, and much more.

9.4. Insights from Analytics-Driven Growth

Let us now delve into the benefits of analytics and data-driven growth:

1. **Understanding Audience Behavior:** It helps you comprehend characteristics of your audience like their age, gender, the region they come from, their preferred content type, time they are most active, and their typical behavior on your posts.

2. **Content Optimization:** Analytics judiciously informs decisions about content creation, including the type, tone, relevance, and timing of posts, leading to better engagement and followership.

3. **Competitor Analysis:** Stay ahead of the curve by using analytics to track competitor activities, audience growth, trending hashtags, and popular topics in your niche.

4. **Performance Tracking:** It lets you monitor your progress over

time, providing a wider perspective on your strategy's success or failure.

5. **Crisis Detection:** Analytics can bring potential issues to light before they escalate into significant problems, by monitoring dips in engagement, negative sentiment, or sudden changes in follower counts.

9.5. From Data to Action: The Analyze and Iterate Cycle

Once you have the data at hand, the real game begins. Draw inferences from the data, implement changes in your strategy based on these insights, and then measure the impact of these changes through continued analysis. This Grow-Analyze-Repeat loop is the lifeblood of any data-driven strategy.

In conclusion, while navigating through the tumultuous waves of social media, analytics serves as your compass, guiding you towards your destination. While it may seem daunting at first, remember, it's not about the amount of data you have, but how you use it. So, make social media analytics your best ally, and experience the transformation in your digital journey.

Chapter 10. Crisis Management: Navigating Through Digital Storms

Navigating the stormy seas of digital crises, whether they rise from negative reviews, detrimental rumors, or customer complaints, can often feel like an arduous endeavor. The powerful aspect of social media comes with a double-edge, and on the flip side resides the potential for crises to spiral out of control with alarming speed.

10.1. Understanding Digital Crises

Any sensitive or controversial issue that reaches public attention via social media channels can be classified as a digital crisis. It's essential to comprehend the nature and dynamics of digital crises to effectively manage them. Digital crises can range from complaints by disgruntled customers, product/service failures, damaging press coverage, to cybersecurity breaches. One common thread linking all of these is how speedily they can spread in a connected world, thereby threatening to destabilize your brand's online identity.

10.2. Role of a Crisis Management Plan

A robust crisis management plan forms the cornerstone of any business's digital survival strategy. This blueprint acts as your guide, detailing step-by-step procedures for handling situations effectively and efficiently. The plan should encompass internal communication strategies, assigning roles and responsibilities, and a hierarchy of response procedures. Remember, the goal of a crisis management plan is to ensure swift response, clear communication, and effective mitigation of damage caused by the crisis.

10.3. Identifying the Crisis

The first step in crisis management entails identifying and acknowledging the crisis. Quick identification and prompt acknowledgment can initiate the process of controlling the narrative. Monitor your brand mentions, customer reviews, and comments across all digital platforms. Utilize cutting-edge sentiment analysis tools available today to pick up the minutest negative connotations that can potentially snowball into a massive crisis.

10.4. Framing an Appropriate Response

Upon identifying and understanding the nature of the crisis, it's time to frame an appropriate response. Applying the "STOP" approach can be highly beneficial - 'Sorry, Thank the complainant, Offer a solution, and Promise to do better.'

10.5. Communicating the Response

Crafting a response is just the tip of the iceberg; communicating it effectively is the challenging part. Be sure to use a tone that aligns with your brand values. Transparency, humility, and sincerity should be the pillars supporting your message. While a public acknowledgment can demonstrate your responsibility, personal responses will reflect empathy and commitment towards redressal.

10.6. Learning from the Crisis

Every crisis offers an opportunity to learn and grow. Analyze the various stages of the crisis - from its inception to escalation, and finally, resolution. Evaluate what worked and identify areas that need improvement. Each crisis becomes a learning ground to beef up your strategy for future encounters.

10.7. Taking Preventive Measures

The best crisis management plan is one that prevents crises in the first place. Ensure reflections from previous crises translate into practices, policies, and guidelines aimed at prevention. Build a reputation for excellent customer service and promote transparency to secure trust, thereby minimizing the possibility of a crisis.

Navigating through digital storms can often feel daunting. However, with a robust crisis management plan, prompt recognition, an appropriate response, and a learning mindset, your business can successfully sail through the unpredictable digital landscape. The key lies in maintaining calm, ensuring a clear line of action, and approaching situations with a 'crisis as opportunity' mindset—allowing your brand to emerge stronger, wiser, and more confident than ever before.

Chapter 11. Looking Ahead: Future Trends & Your Social Media Readiness

In the realm of the digital world, where social media reigns supreme, it is important to not just understand the present, but also cast an eagle's gaze into what lies ahead in the increasingly intricate landscape of likes, share, and retweets. This chapter will provide a comprehensive analysis of the emerging trends that are set to shape the future of social media and discuss how you, as an entrepreneur, can prepare your business and strategize effectively to match the pace of this rapidly evolving sphere.

11.1. Preparing for the AI Revolution

A game-changer already sending ripples through the social media sphere, Artificial Intelligence (AI) is predicted to revolutionize the way we approach and navigate social media in the near future. AI's most significant implication lies in its potential to bring unprecedented personalization, with algorithms designed to deliver content tailored specifically to individual preferences and behaviors. This means that businesses need to invest in understanding and implementing AI to ensure their content remains relevant and reaches the right audiences.

But AI is not solely about personalization. It's also about understanding and engaging with audiences on a deeper level. Chatbots and conversational AI are increasingly being used to enhance customer service on social media platforms. They provide immediate, accurate responses to customer queries and can engage users in a more personable manner, creating a better user experience. Plan to integrate these tools into your customer engagement strategy to ensure a consistent and superior customer experience.

11.2. Riding the Video and Visual Content Wave

Video has already proven to be a powerful content format on social media, and its dominance is expected to continue to grow. Live streaming, in particular, has gained considerable momentum, offering real-time interaction and improving the connection between brands and followers. This type of content invites audiences into the world of the brand instantly and authentically, proving incredibly potent for fostering relationships and building trust.

Visual content is not just limited to video, though. The rising popularity of ephemeral content, like Stories on Instagram and Facebook, presents a unique opportunity to deliver quick and Personable snippets about your brand. Carefully curated visuals and exciting infographics also remain profoundly engaging in the ever-swirling feeds of the followers.

11.3. Embracing the World of Augmented Reality, Virtual Reality, and Mixed Reality

Social platforms are increasingly exploring Augmented Reality (AR), Virtual Reality (VR), and Mixed Reality (MR) to provide immersive experiences. Brands that can leverage these technologies to create interactive and engaging experiences will have an edge over competitors. Providing AR filters related to your brand, creating immersive VR content to promote your products, or using MR to engage with your community can yield high return on investments by creating unique user experiences and driving engagement.

11.4. Tapping into the Power of User-Generated Content and Influencer Collaborations

User-Generated Content (UGC) and collaborations with influencers are looking to play even more substantial roles in the social media strategies of brands. UGC, essentially content created by users about a brand or product, offers a way to tap into the digital word-of-mouth phenomenon. Build initiatives that encourage followers to share their experiences with your brand or products in return for rewards or recognition. Furthermore, partnering with influencers, especially micro-influencers, can offer high engagement rates and increase your brand's reach to new audiences.

11.5. Leveraging Social Commerce

Social Commerce, buying and selling directly on social media platforms, is becoming an integral part of social media marketing. The convenience it offers to users to shop without having to leave their favorite social platform is attractive and boosts sales. Keep an eye on this trend and start planning how to integrate your product catalogue within social media platforms like Facebook, Instagram, and Pinterest.

11.6. Integrating Social Listening and Analytics

Social Listening and analytics is rapidly evolving, giving businesses even more insights and data about their audience's behaviors, feelings, and preferences. Advanced analytics can help understand the emotional responses to your brand's posts, improving the understanding of your audience and helping shape future content strategy. Building up your capabilities in social listening and analytics can offer substantial advantages in fine-tuning your social media strategy and improving your engagement rates.

While some of these trends might feel overwhelming, remember that you don't need to integrate all of them at once. Prioritize based on what fits best with your brand's DNA and what will resonate most with your audience. Start experimenting today to prepare for the social media landscape of tomorrow. The world of social media is fast-paced and ever-changing. By keeping a vigilant eye on emerging trends and adjusting your strategy to meet these transformations, your brand can ride the wave of the future and secure its space in the digital realm. The key is to stay adaptable and continue learning. Stay proactive in your approach and soon, the fluid shifts of the digital waves will be less intimidating and more of an invigorating challenge. Your readiness for these future trends is essential to maintain a strong presence and to outperform competitors in the ever-evolving social media playground.